THE ART
OF EMPLOYEE
RELATIONS

Overcoming Your Fear of Addressing Employee Issues

Deborah A Tullos

THE ART OF EMPLOYEE RELATIONS
Overcoming Your Fear of Addressing
Employee Issues

ISBN: 9798673138113 (Paperback)

Contact the Author:

Deborahatullos@gmail.com

THE ART OF EMPLOYEE RELATIONS

Overcoming Your Fear of Addressing Employee Issues

Deborah A. Tullos

Acknowledgement

I thank all the managers and employees who have allowed me to be a part of their lives and trusting me to help resolve their concerns.

I also thank my fellow human resources professional, who served as sounding boards during the resolution of some, particularly difficult issues.

A special thank you to my family and friends for their encouragement during this project.

Table of Content

Introduction

My professional human resources career provided me the opportunity to work with managers at all levels within organizations. I have been privileged to witness them struggle with managing people and addressing their issues. With help, some embraced the necessary skills, and became successful and effective leaders; some chose to follow the examples set for them by previous managers and moved down the winding road of "management through intimidation", while others crossed to the other side of the bridge of "management by avoidance."

Every manager who has had a desire to be a better leader has probably looked for a book, article, or workshop to give them the secrets to success in managing people. Based upon the number of books that are available in the market, I'm sure many of those managers were able to find and internalize some of this information and make some improvements in their management abilities. Unfortunately, this is not true for the majority of managers who after completing their reading, were sadly left with a "so what do I do now" feeling.

The manager, struggling with difficult and sometimes confusing issues, needs to have the "right" information at the "right" time, presented in the "right" way to be useful when dealing with the day-to-day management of people.

That need was the impetus for the writing of this book. **The Art of Employee Relations** is designed to give the new and experienced manager the "just in time" support needed to address and resolve employee issues in the workplace by offering a different perceptive from which to approach performance issues. This book deals less with the legal and policy aspects of workplace concerns, but more about people and how to approach these people issues. This book provides information on the "Artistic" aspect of the

"Practice" of employee relations. The "Practice" of employee relations is focused on organizational policies and employment and discrimination laws. Those policies and laws can be found in your organization's intranet or policy manuals. Employment laws can be found on the Department of Labor website and will not be discussed in this book.

This book is dedicated to developing the "Artist" in each manager preparing them to create the best possible human interactions. It deals with how to finesse difficult encounters to create positive outcomes. It focuses on how to use what is considered the "soft skills" to guide the conversation in the direction that would be most productive. It provides an approach that will help address and enhance the working relationship or if necessary, ends the working relationship in a way that does not demean and devalue the separating employee. Examples of employee issues are also included. They are intended to assist in developing vital people management skills.

The Art of Employee Relations is divided into two parts. Part 1 is intended to define the role of the manager, establish the foundation of effective leadership through the mastering ten foundations that I call the Fundamentals of Management. Part 2 explains the Calm Approach, which is an effective technique that I have created to master most interactions with employees. It provides step-by-step instructions designed to guide managers through the difficult day-to-day discussions with employees such as poor performance, conflicts in the workplace, time and attendance issues, and inappropriate behaviours. Part 2 also includes effective techniques to address unique performance situations.

Through the materials provided in this book, you will find that effective people management skills can be learned and like other business management skills, these skills can only be improved and become more natural with practice.

"Coming together is the beginning. Keeping together is progress. Working together is success." - Henry Ford.

PART ONE

Chapter 1

THE ROLE OF THE MANAGER

As a manager in your organization, you are expected to work hard to help your organization reach established goals. Many organizations have documented in their goals, as a desire to strive toward greatness. But this greatness can only be achieved through great leaders.

To be a great leader, you must take the responsibilities of leadership and self-development seriously. As a manager, at some point in your development, you must have the courage to make an honest assessment of your leadership abilities. It is only through this honest assessment that you will be able to determine whether you have the necessary skills and the fortitude to become the great leader that you desire to be.

For example, how would you answer the following questions?

- How effective are you at expressing your thoughts?

- Do you trust your knowledge of the area(s) that you are held accountable for?

- Do you avoid situations that you think may cause you to become tense or confrontational?

- Are you uncomfortable explaining your decision to other leaders in your organization?

- Are you able to stand behind your decisions when others try to persuade you to change your mind, or when you know that your decision is in the best interest of the organization or for your staff?

If these questions usher in conflicting emotions,

don't be overly concerned. Your honest response to these questions may have revealed the one thing that you hoped would stay hidden. The one thing that you hoped would stay hidden is the feeling of fear. Fear is a normal response when you find yourself in unfamiliar or uncomfortable situations.

Fear is what influences managers to avoid addressing employee issues. Fear is what causes managers to allow employees to misbehave in the workplace. Fear is what drives managers to remain silent when they know they should speak up. Fear is what drives some managers to become tyrants in the workplace, unwilling to acknowledge other's opinions. Fear permits managers to settle for mediocrity when greatness is what they desire.

Don't be disheartened. This fear can be overcome with knowledge and preparation. Overcoming fear begins with becoming grounded in the basics of management. The discovery that I made while serving in the field was that the lack of preparation and training of managers in how to address issues with employees was what established this type of fear. It did not matter whether it was a new manager, middle manager, or senior-level manager, the availability of information and accountability for professional growth was sadly lacking. I found that new managers did not know what to ask, middle managers, preferred to hide the fact that they did not know how to address issues, because of fear of being embarrassed. The majority of senior managers believed that because they had already arrived at their position in the organization, they did not need to expand their knowledge of how to address and resolve employee issues.

These basics are a collection of practices that I found to be a universal need while working with struggling managers. I refer to these practices as the Fundamentals of Management. Mastering these foundational practices will give you the confidence you need to address any employee issues and stand by your decisions.

Chapter 2

FUNDAMENTALS OF MANAGEMENT

Do not assume that you will master these fundamentals immediately. The mastery of these fundamentals will take time, attention, study, and practice. Some you will need to practice throughout your professional career while they slowly begin to feel natural to you. The most important goal at this point is simply to be aware that these fundamentals exist.

So, take your time. Read through them slowly, pause when a particular statement touches on an experience that has impacted you. Consider how you may have given a different response to the situation.

Let's begin:

1. Managers must have a thorough knowledge of federal, state laws, and organizational policies and practices related to the management of employees.

Most managers believe that they don't need to know and understand employment policies. They believe those items are the responsibility of Human Resources and all they need to do is refer the employee to Human Resources or call the Human Resources department themselves as the need arises. Unfortunately, that attitude can get a manager in big trouble. Without knowledge of discrimination laws, protected groups, and prohibited actions, the manager leaves himself and his organization vulnerable to significant legal actions.

Internal company policies can vary in each organization that a manager has been employed. It is vital to review the common policies of attendance, disciplinary actions, dress codes, and leaves, to ensure that your department remains in compliance.

Exercise:

Make a list and review all employment laws and organizational policies that pertain to the hiring, promotions, restrictions, discriminations, infractions, pay, evaluations, and discipline. Refer to your organization's policy manual and the Department of Labor website for this information.

This action does not require that you become an expert on employment law, but rather that you become aware of their existence.

2. Managers must understand the technical aspects of their assigned departments.

It would be great if we could always manage those areas for which we have the expertise, but there are times when due to budget constraints or reorganizations, we are called upon to be responsible for areas for which we have limited knowledge.

The temptation is to just rely on the staff working in that area to do what is necessary and meet whatever departmental goals that have already been established. Unfortunately, that rarely happens. An effective leader needs to take the time and do his/her homework. The manager needs to understand the essential functions of the assigned area, the stakeholders, the areas of vulnerability, the past successes and failures, budget requirements, who the superstars are in the area, as well as, the slackers.

This investment of time serves several purposes. Firstly, the manager gains knowledge about his new assignments and the confidence that goes along with having an understanding of these new expectations. Secondly, this approach lets organizational leaders know that these new responsibilities are being taken seriously and that as a manager you plan on putting forth your best effort to manage the new areas. Thirdly, you gain the respect of your newly assigned staff, by demonstrating that you have an interest in what they do. And last, but not least, you can effectively manage the new staff because you know how to evaluate whether they are producing at the rate to meet the desired goals.

Exercise:

Create an electronic table of your assigned areas. List the responsibilities, goals, deadlines, current efficiency status, stakeholders and department challenges.

Use this table to monitor and document department activities and progress.

Take the time to talk to the staff to understand

their duties, challenges, frustrations, and motivations.

3. Managers must maintain confidentiality.

One of the main issues that can erode the relationship between the manager and the employee is when the employee feels that the manager cannot be trusted with information pertaining to them. This can be information related to their job performance, disciplinary actions, health concerns, or family issues. In the employee's mind, if the manager will discuss one employee's performance or personal information with another employee, they believe at some point their personal information is also at risk.

Exercise:
Make a point to treat all employee information with the greatest discretion. Even if the employee decides to discuss their issues with co-workers, as a manager it is not proper to

discuss these issues with anyone other than the employee or human resources official only if it is necessary.

    4. Managers must be able to separate friendships from organizational responsibilities.

As humans in the workplace, we all have individuals that we like more than others. In some cases, a manager may even share an established relationship with an employee. There are times when these individuals that we've become friends with work in areas that fall under our scope of responsibilities. This supervisor/subordinate situation can create strains on the friendship, the department, and the coworkers in the areas.

When a friend is responsible for managing a friend, other employees automatically assume that the friend will receive preferential treatment. They assume the friend will be held to a different standard, be allowed more leniency when it comes to work-time requirements, holidays and vacations, deadlines, and behavior. They assume the friend will always have the manager's ear when change is made and when conflict occurs. The effective manager needs to address this concern head-on. The best approach is to have a conversation with a friend to establish a clear understanding of the separation between friendship and work expectations. The friend should then be held to the same standard as others in the department. Any deviation will be detrimental to the workplace.

Exercise:

Open communication regarding friendships is vital. Boundaries must be established regarding attendance, tardiness, workplace conversations, and acceptable behaviors. Continuing these outside friendships after becoming a manager may at some point be called into question. The phrase that I use is "it's good until it's not". If the friendship at

some point goes sour, potentially all of the secrets you shared with that person will become kindling workplace fires.

5. Managers must be objective.

A manager must be willing to accept information from a variety of sources and make decisions that are in the best interest of the organization. There is the temptation to only listen to those individuals who have been a part of the organization for an extended time or those individuals that you have established friendships with.   Remember that while these individuals may provide you with valuable information, employees new to the organization or department, or those who may have firsthand knowledge may be able to provide you with the missing pieces of the puzzle.

Exercise:

Interview a variety of people who may be reluctant to speak on an issue, but they have

firsthand information regarding the situation. Look to those individuals who rarely comment or rarely come forward with information. Usually, these people are observers who will only respond to inquiries that are made directly to them.

6. Managers must stress accountability for themselves and their staff.

Managers must be willing to hold themselves to the highest of standards. The most difficult thing that an individual can do is to be objective about him/herself. Attempting to see yourself as others see you takes courage. What would others see when they observe how you manage your time, how you pay attention to your attire, your actions, behavior, conversations, and conduct?

Exercise:

As a manager, you must avoid the "do as I say and not as I do approach". Accountability

includes reporting to work on time, maintaining your appearance, not abusing leave time, exhibiting a positive attitude, and treating everyone with dignity and respect.

7. Managers must be able to control their own emotions and not take personal frustrations in their interactions with others.

Frustrations in life happen to everyone, A manager must be able to control those frustrations. It is vital to your success in your role. Employees look to their managers to set the daily tone in the work environment. The tone should be consistently positive and not have the employees feeling as if they have to walk on eggshells wondering what mood their manager will be in daily.

Exercise:

Before entering your office each day, allow yourself one minute to take calming breathes and focus your mind on the day's activities.

Release any home-related frustrations that could impact your interactions with your staff. If you are new to the department, remember that members of your new team are not replacements for our previous team. Take the time to get to know each person.

8. Managers must show respect for staff and other organizational leaders.

A manager should never allow himself to fall into the trap of believing that he is superior to the people that he manages or superior to the other leaders in the organization. The manager should respect everyone in the workplace for the role that they play in meeting the company's goals. The respect should apply to everyone from the cleaning staff to the C-suite leaders. Undermining an employee or fellow manager reflects more on the person doing the undermining than the intended target.

Exercise:

Practice interacting with everyone that you encounter with a sincere hello. This action will allow you to appear more approachable to staff and other managers in the organization. Just that simple act over time will allow others to see you positively.

9. Managers must be committed to coaching and developing their staff.

It's not enough to be a manager, you must become a leader of others. Take the time to invest in the people that you manage. Be a teacher, guide others to be successful by not only pointing out the areas that they need to improve, but also the areas in which they excel. Use positive feedback to encourage your staff to always do their best. Look for untapped skills in employees that can be developed for use by the organization.

Exercise:

Begin by selecting one employee to practice positive reinforcement. Pay attention to their response. You will notice how the employee will work harder by becoming more focused on the small aspects of their responsibilities to receive more positive feedback.

10. Managers must enforce the rules of their organization regardless of their thoughts or how insignificant they may think the rules are.

When working for organizations, you won't always agree with the policies that have been established. When you accepted the role of manager, you accepted more than just a title. You accepted the role of being a representative of the organization to which you are employed. As such, any decision or comment that you make, you make on behalf of the organization. Legally, by supporting the organization's policies you are protected from any adverse actions.   However, if you act in contradiction to the organization's policies or make derogatory comments about the organization's policies or actions, you open yourself up to legal actions for which you can be held personally responsible.

Exercise:
When you encounter organizational policies that you are confused/unclear about, or that you disagree with, contact your Human Resources department to discuss the policy. They will help you to understand the background of the policy or the legal issues that impact the organization's position.

These Fundamentals of Management are the minimum necessary components that will prepare you to become a valuable leader in your organization.

Embracing these fundaments along with the other information provided in this book will move you closer to overcoming your fear of addressing any employee workplace issues.

Three things cannot be long hidden: the sun, the moon, and the truth. - The Buddha.

PART TWO

Chapter 3

THE CALM APPROACH

In my professional role, I frequently supported managers by sitting with them during critical conversations with employees. One comment that I heard repeatedly about that support was my ability to appear calm during stressful interactions. Many managers commented that during tense situations with employees they were amazed that my demeanor never changed. They marveled at my ability to not get drawn into the emotions of the situation that was taking place before us. They would openly share how they had to use every ounce of restraint to not lash out at the employee or refute some of the things that were being said. After many of these intense meetings, managers thanked me for the little pat on the leg or the small tap on their shoe. These actions had become my habit of offering a reminder to the manager that they needed to stay composed. A reminder that they needed to hold their peace while the employee was making statements that they felt were untrue or misinterpreted. That tap was my communication to them that I sensed their frustrations rising or that their demeanor had started to change.

In part, my appearance of having a calm demeanor comes from my extensive training in conflict management techniques, but I must confess that it is also my normal state of being. I am an observer of people and I am frequently fascinated by the behaviors and lengths that people are willing to go to get their points across and their opinions heard. That fascination has to lead me to study to receive an undergraduate degree in Social Science with a concentration in Psychology, and later to earn a Master's degree in Behavioral Science with a focus on Negotiation and Conflict Management.

Don't be alarmed if you do not possess an innate ability to manage your emotions. You can learn to stay in control during these tense employee situations. You can learn to push down that queasy feeling of anticipation and keep it from overtaking you. You can suppress that "fight or flight" reflex that is urging you to leave the area instead of staying to deal with the duty at hand.

In this section, I will give you the tools that will help you to work through your inner conflict and prepare you to address any employee situation that confronts you. By using this tool, you will be able to confidently address issues related to time and attendance, poor customer service, inappropriate behavior, theft, or any other issue, with calm and finesse. This approach has worked for me, for the past 20 years and I know that it will work for you.   I present to you the C.A.L.M. Approach.

***

The two key elements that will determine your success when using the C.A.L.M Approach are **listening** and **tone.**

Listening involves more than words!
Of course, it's important to pay attention to the words that are being communicated, but to understand more about what the employee is attempting to tell you, you must also pay attention to several other factors.
When the employee is speaking, give them your undivided attention. Watch their body movements. Are they standing, sitting, or gesturing? If sitting, are they leaning forward or are they sitting back in the seat?
Each movement can give you more insight into the emotions and motivations of the employee. Understand that these actions are not planned

displays by the employee. They are outward expressions of their internal conflicts.

Standing can reveal that the employee wants to be in control and is unwilling to show any degree of compromise. If the employee is pacing the floor, this employee is feeling trapped and is waiting for an opportunity to leave the room.

If sitting, sitting back in the seat suggests that the employee is guarded and waiting for what may come next. Sitting forward in the seat, lets you know that the employee may be nervous, but that they are alert.

If the employee is using excessive gesturing, they may be trying to distract your attention from the conversation.

Taken in consideration with the body language, the volume, and rhythm in which the employee is speaking can also reveal a great deal. Loud and rapid talking is another control strategy. Soft-spoken and slow-paced speech may mean that the employee is unsure or being untruthful.

There are rapport building strategies, such as

mirroring and pacing, that can be used to respond to each of these unconscious behaviors. I won't include training on these techniques in this book, but introduce the topic to encourage you to explore if you have an interest.

A word of caution.

If you feel that the employee's behavior has escalated to a level that you cannot manage, end the conversation immediately and leave the room! Some employees have issues that are beyond the training of the manager or the employee relations professional and should be referred or encouraged to seek help from the Employee Assistance Program.

'Tone' is the second key element!

Having the proper tone is a vital part of this approach. The tone of voice that you use when speaking with people will either draw them to you or push them away. Tone can either move an employee to strive for greatness or move them to walk away. Tone can make you an approachable and talented leader or cause your career to end before it has had time to develop.

At this point you are probably asking yourself several questions. What I mean by tone? How would you go about finding it? How will you know if your tone is correct?

Recall if you will, a time when someone you care about took the time to share something important with you. Or, a time when someone took the time to teach you how to cook, cut, build, sew, catch, whatever. Or when you took the time to do the same for someone else.

Reflect on the experience and the tone that the person used to draw you in and hold your attention. Or, the tone that you used to explain in detail the step by step instructions of a task.

I imagine that the tone used and the interaction was soft, patient, and slow. Now, think of a time when you were the teacher of a child, parent, or friend. Reflect on the tone that you used to draw that person in and hold their attention. Was your interaction with that person soft, patient, and slow? That is the tone that you must use when dealing with employee relation issues. Even if you have a dozen other concerns that you need to address, the interaction that you are having at that moment, with that employee has to come across to the employee as the most important thing that you are dealing with that day. The meeting may only last for 15 to 20 minutes, but that time should be devoted exclusively to the employee and the issue at hand.

***

The following four steps of the Calm Approach will provide you with the guidance you need to address most workplace issues.

STEP 1:

C- Clear your mind of pre-conceived judgments

As humans, we all have people that we interact with better, or that we respond to more positively. A casual meeting in a checkout line or a conversation during a brief flight can leave you feeling as though you've known that person for a much longer time. During that brief interaction, you were able to establish a connection. At another time, a glance at a stranger who reminds you of a distrusted person from your past can have you passing judgment on that person without even a hello. With this person, you avoid making a connection.

As a manager, when it is necessary to speak with an employee, it is necessary to put aside any personal feelings or thoughts that you may have toward the employee to resolve the issue at hand. We've all heard the saying, "even paranoids have enemies". It may be true that this particular employee has been your "problem child" in the past, it does not mean that the issue being discussed in this meeting is of their making. When you approach the employee without any pre-conceived judgments, you will be able to discuss the issue, view, and receive any information with "fresh eyes and ears".

STEP 2

A-Allow the employee to tell their story

When the employee begins to speak, allow them to speak their truth as they see it. Don't interrupt, don't correct, and don't reprimand, simply allow the individual to speak. During the time that the employee is speaking, you should be taking notes. These notes can be used to ask questions after the employee has finished speaking. They can also be used to validate the information that was shared. What the employee will perceive is (1) that you are interested in what they have to say, (2) you are making notes so you will be able to follow up on what they are saying, and (3) if they say something that is not the truth, you have documented the conversation and they know that they will be accountable in the future.

Everyone wants to be heard. Your effort of taking notes communicates to the employee that they have something valuable to say and that you are interested enough to write it down.

Most employees are nervous when asked to have a conversation with their manager. Some become defensive and angry even before they know what the details of the meeting involve. If the employee is hostile, do not allow yourself to follow suit. Let the employee know that you are available and willing to hear what they have to say, but that you want to make sure first that they understand what the most pressing issue is. At this point, the employee will usually pause to allow you to introduce the topic of the discussion.

Don't be alarmed if at some point the employee begins to cry. In my experience, employees cry for two reasons. One reason is out of frustration of believing that they have been wronged or out of the relief having the opportunity to be heard.

Many employees have shared with me that they didn't feel like they were being heard when they talked. They felt that managers came to the meeting with the preconceived judgments, and disciplinary documents in hand, merely looking for the signature on the bottom line. When the employee feels that someone is listening, the relief of being heard often moves them to tears.

There is a small group of employees who completely shut done when conflicted with any type of issue or discussion. Interface with such employees requires a great deal of patience. As a manager, your role with this employee is to not rush to fill in the silence. Ask the employee a question and then wait for the answer. If after several minutes the employee has not been forthcoming, ask what they are thinking and why they have chosen to become quiet. This will usually get the employee talking. Explore this area with the employee for a few minutes and then you can return to the topic at hand.

Even if at the end of the conversation the disciplinary document is presented, the employee walks away feeling as if regardless of that fact, they were finally listened to and are more apt to acknowledge their role in the situation.

STEP 3:

L -Listen for Details

While the person is speaking, listen for relevant details. If the issue is time and attendance, listen for details that may open up a conversation about flexible scheduling, alternate schedules, FMLA concerns, temporary child care issues, adult care issues, transportation issues, or simply, that the person just does not care and believes that the party can only start when they show up.

If the issue is behavior, listen for details about their interactions with others, how long they've been in their role; they may have gotten comfortable and started to insert "home" behavior into their work environment. After allowing the person to share their side of the situation an effective strategy is to ask the person to describe and share how they get along at home when things become stressful. This will give a clearer picture of who the person is and their "go-to" behavior in stressful situations. Most employees are not able to separate the behaviors that they are comfortable with from the expectations that they are confronted with within the workplace.

STEP 4:

M- Maintain dignity

Maintaining the dignity of the employee and the situation is probably the most important step in the CALM APPROACH. You can communicate sensitive or difficult information to an employee in a way that they will receive it if they know that you value them as a person and an employee. Do not talk down to the employee and do not blame others for you taking the actions that you decide to take. Maintaining the tone that we discussed earlier, speak directly to the employee, and share the expectations that you have to resolve the issue. Include any follow-up actions or monitoring that the employee will undergo.

Chapter 4

PREPARING FOR THE CONVERSATION

- This is a performance issue
- This is a behavioral issue

The performance issue is:

____

____

____

____

____

____

____

The behavioral issue is:

____

____

____

____

____

____

The change that needs to occur is:

____

____

____

____

____

____

After you have determined whether you are dealing with a performance or behavioral issue and what is the best resolution, you are ready to invite the employee to have a conversation.

Arrange the meeting for a time when you are less likely to be distracted with other people or issues. Make sure that the location for the meeting is in a private space that cannot be overheard by others.

Be aware that most employees are very nervous when asked to meet with their supervisor, so be prepared that the employee will hesitate to meet with you.

If you have considered carefully the information presented to this point in the book, you are now prepared to engage in a conversation with your employee and work toward resolving the pressing issue.

- Remember the Fundamentals of Management
- Assess the situation.
- Remember to apply the Calm Approach

Above all, remember that the goal is to resolve the issue and to maintain the relationship. Even if the resolution is to separate the employee, this approach maintains the dignity of the employee and displays a level of respect for the individual that usually prevents hostility.

Chapter 5

CONVERSATION STARTERS

Many managers confessed that their greatest fear was how to begin the conversation with an employee about a work-related issue.

Beginning the conversation incorrectly can send the interaction into a downward direction that may be difficult to recover. An incorrect approach would be one in which you open the conversation announcing the outcome of the meeting or by accusing the employee.

However, beginning the conversation correctly can lead to buy-in by the employee, and a positive resolution of the issue. This can enhance the working relationship between the manager and the employee.

Beginning the conversation with the employee is just an extension of the preparation that has already been done.

You should have reviewed behavior related reports of any investigation conducted and any witness-statements submitted. You should have reviewed the employee's attendance record if attendance is the issue. If job performance is the issue, you should have reviewed any notes or file for job performance counseling documents, emails, performance improvement plans, or previous disciplinary actions.

You want to be as prepared as possible before engaging the employee in a conversation. I cannot count the number of times when called to intervene in situations with employees - I was told that when they had a discussion (s) with their manager, the manager had not collected the details about the situation before they were brought in to discuss.

Using the same approach for all employee relations issues is not appropriate and can come across to the employee as being insincere. Different employee issues require different introductory statements that are geared toward the issue and the individual.

It would be impossible to try to script every issue that a manager may encounter with an employee, so for this book, only the most common employee critical conversations will be addressed.

The examples can be modified to address other employee situations.

Example 1: Attendance

If the issue involves attendance (absences or tardiness) the recommended introductory statement used maybe something along these lines.

"A review of your time records shows an

excessive amount of absences/tardiness. We need to discuss the impact of your attendance record and what changes you need to make or what we can do as an organization to help you get back on track."

With this approach, you have put the employee on notice that their attendance is unacceptable, but you are open and willing to discuss possible solutions to the attendance problem.

The employee may have gotten lax in their morning schedule or they may be experiencing unforeseen issues that have impacted their ability to get to work on time.

Example 2: Employee Complaint

If the issue involves a complaint of some type, the recommended introductory statement used maybe something along these lines.

"It was brought to our attention that you may have witnessed or been involved in a negative interaction with (could be a co-worker, patient, customer, family member).

We would like to hear what you know and get your side of the situation."

With this approach, you are not blaming the employee for any inappropriate actions, but rather, you are allowing the employee to present the information in their own words.

Example 3: Investigations

If the issue involves information discovered during an investigation of some type, the recommended introductory statement used maybe something along these lines.

> *"As a result of an on-going investigation, we received information that involves you. We would like to ask you a few questions and gather any information from you that will help complete our investigation into this matter."*

At this point, without revealing to the employee what the investigation is about, you have put them on notice that you have done your homework and you already have details about the issue involved. Believe me, the employee's mind will begin spinning in all directions and recalling all the incidences that could be revealed.

From this point, you can reveal to the employee the essence of the investigation and document their response.

Example 4: Job Performance

If the issue involves an issue of poor job performance, whether, for a newly hired employee or an on-going issue, the recommended introductory statement used maybe something along these lines.

> *"I set aside this time to talk about the feedback I've received so far about your job performance. There are some areas that you seem to be doing well in, but there are other areas that we need to make sure you are getting the support that you need to be successful.*
>
> *Let's discuss the things that you are doing well, then we can discuss what kind of support you need to improve in the other*

areas."

Telling the employee upfront that you set aside time to have a discussion lets the employee know that they are valued as an employee. Noting the good performance and areas of improvement, lets the employee know that you have been paying attention to the job that they have been doing.

The most effective way of getting an employee's performance moving in the right direction is to invest time and attention in the employee. You may need to arrange retraining or monitoring to ensure that the employee stays on track. The main thing is to stay in touch with and tuned to the employee's needs and performance.

Chapter 6

I UNDERSTAND......
HOWEVER

It's been said that the story resides in the dash. Such is the case here. Whenever I am asked what advice I would offer managers in response to dealing with employee issues, I would usually recommend these words, "I understand…. however,". As previously stated, when engaging in conversations with employees, it's important to provide them the opportunity to express their thoughts and to give their side of the situation. It is equally important for the manager to respond to the statements made by the employee and to address the response from their perspective, and based on their role in the organization.

I UNDERSTAND – HOWEVER is the single most effective response that I believe equips the manager to address the employee's most pressing issue. But remember, I said that the story resides in the dash. What is said between the words I UNDERSTAND and the HOWEVER will determine whether the employee will listen to what follows.

Using the words, I UNDERSTAND should be followed by a summary of the information that the employee shared during their time to speak. (Example, I understand that you have been late every day for the past month because your mother has recently moved in with you and you have to prepare things for her before you leave for work.)

Provide as much detail as the employee shared with you. This lets the employee know that you were listening to their explanation and value the time that it took for them to share. Watch the employee's response. You will notice that the employee is actively listening to your response because you are voicing their words. When you have finished with your paraphrasing of their explanation move to the next step.

Now is the time to use the word, HOWEVER. HOWEVER, signals to the employee that there may have been a flaw in their logic. The words that follow, HOWEVER, is your opportunity to reinforce the expectation of your organization. (Referring to the previous example, I understand that you have been late every day for the past month because of your need to prepare things for your mother. HOWEVER, in the offer letter that you signed, you agreed that you would be available during the hours listed. Is that correct?

At this point, you can talk through options that may be available to the employee from the Employee Assistance Program, or a temporary change of schedule, even to walking through what preparations the employee can make to allow the employee to be on time for work.

Be prepared. At any time during this critical conversation, the employee's behavior may change. The employee may escalate their behavior or they may shut down and stop talking altogether. Guard yourself against your natural inclination to follow the employee in this escalation. Instead, remain calm and work to focus the employee on the issue at hand.

The goal is to get the employee to understand the importance of them fulfilling their responsibility to the organization as well as their other obligations.

Chapter 7

UNDERSTAND THE SITUATION AND DETERMINE THE GOAL

There are times when unique opportunities present themselves and the efforts to resolve the conflict requires the use of creative methods. Each situation has some twist that is different from the one before it. To be successful, you must be able to assess the situation and understand the role that each participant played in the creation of the conflict.

Much of the knowledge needed to address conflict we already have. As humans, we know how to push each other's buttons and how to hold our tongues in order not to hurt someone's feelings. We've learned how to build people up and how to tear down.

The art of employee relations involves using knowledge of human behavior to build employees up and set them on the right course; not to tear them down or devalue them. It involves using the knowledge that you have or will gather regarding the employee(s) involved in the situation to achieve the best outcome.

So, do the work. Take into account, as much as possible, the personalities, the background, and the performance history of the parties involved. Try never to walk into a situation without an understanding of what is involved, what is at stake, and what the outcome needs to be.

If the situation is more pressing and time does not allow you to gather the background information ahead of time, move to deescalate the situation without resolution. Separate the parties. Remove them from the premises, if necessary, until the data can be gathered and recommendations formulated.

Although each situation and each person are different the path that you take to find a resolution for the issues will always incorporate the steps presented in this book. Each path will bring you to the point of having a face-to-face conversation with the employee. Each path will allow you to listen to the employee's side of the story, and allow you the opportunity to set or reset the expectations of the employee.

Follow up is key to the success of any of these strategies. Avoid giving the impression that you are not interested in the resolution of the issue. Periodic check-ins will let the employee know that their success is important to you and the organization.

The following are examples of unconventional approaches to situations that proved to be effective.

Chapter 8

CONFLICT RESOLUTION APPROACHES

Department Out of Step

Occasionally, there are entire departments that seem to be out of step with the rest of the organization. This can be identified through employee satisfaction surveys or by a seemingly constant bubbling up of minor issues in the department that don't rise to the level of human resources intervention for disciplinary action. Almost like a student raising his hand in class for attention. In fact, that exactly what it is. It is an indication that something in the department is out of step. The entire department is sending out a cry for help that something is off.

Finding the solution to get the department back on course is not an external remedy. The department is seeking to have a voice. They are seeking to have a voice in the activity of their department.

The manager may believe that they are doing everything they can for their team and are at a loss to understand the discontent. An effective strategy is to create a venue to give the department a voice.

The goal of the approach is to bring cohesion to the department that is not dictated by the manager. An additional goal is to achieve buy-in from the department's members to the ultimate decisions that are made. The best solutions usually come from those who are closest to the issue.

The technique works like this:

Create a task force within the department that includes the most vocal member of the department and the most reserved.

Over several weeks, have the task force, with the help of their non-taskforce department members compile a list of department concerns. Have the taskforce prioritize the list to identify the most pressing department issues.

Next, have the taskforce, again with the help of non-taskforce members, make recommendations to address each concern.

One word of caution. Make it clear that recommendations cannot go against organizational policies or employment or discrimination laws.

Once the list and recommendations have been completed, the task force makes a presentation to the department manager. Managers should immediately implement recommendations that seem appropriate and congratulate the task force and department members for their efforts.

Managers should work toward promptly addressing recommendations that require more time to implement. Any recommendations that are not possible should be explained to the team, to maintain the credibility of the manager with the taskforce.

Role Confusion

Sometimes even managers/directors find themselves struggling to connect with their up line leaders. Each Manager/Director/ Leader comes to their position with preconceived ideas about what the person they report to or what the person they manage should be like. When either fails to meet the image, discord can occur. When they fail to mesh, each can believe that the other is the cause of the conflict. The direct report can feel that the up line is not doing their job and the leader may feel that the direct report is not meeting expectations.

The goal is to get these leaders on the same page.

The following is a technique that has proven to be effective when addressing conflict issues between direct reports and their up line leader.

Arrange a meeting to mediate a conversation with the individuals involved.

Starting with the direct report, ask them to share their perception of what the duties of the up line leader are. Without interruption, allow them to share how they believe the up line has not met that perception.

Next, allow the up line the same opportunity to share their vision and expectations for the role of the direct report.

The differences in expectations should be clear at this point. From this point, the conversation can move to how a shared vision of expectations can be created.

This approach may require several sessions to ensure that negativity is not allowed to enter the process. Re-enforcement of the creation of a team and achieving organizational goals and expectations should be the driving force for this resolution.

Unreasonable Expectations

On rare occasions, there is a need to address concerns with a senior leader of the organization. Many senior leaders are reluctant to listen to or accept criticism of their performance in the organization. Particularly when that criticism may be coming from an individual who they see as at a lower level than they are in the organization. This conversation was tailor-made for the C.A.L.M. Approach.

Employee relations professionals are trained to address issues at whatever level they may be created in the organization. At the senior manager level, respect is the key issue. If the senior manager does not respect the person bringing them the information, they will never accept it. Listen intently to every word that the senior leader shares. Each word will provide clues to the real issues.

In one particular case, as a result of an unfavorable employee survey, an Executive Vice President (EVP) was directed by the Chief Executive Officer (CEO) to meet with me to discuss the results of an employee survey and to create an action plan to improve the department's outcomes.

During the meeting, the EVP was very agitated and defensive for having been placed in the position of having to defend her leadership as department head. She was relentless in her declaration that she would not lower her department's standards to get better survey results. She spent the next three hours explaining all of the dedication and hard work that had gotten her to her current position. She was very focused on how much time and effort her spouse invested in her development.

In this particular situation, it was knowledge of the spouse's investment of time and attention that gave me the opening that I was looking for.

After paraphrasing the EVP's statements, I asked her one question that changed her demeanor. I noted and asked that, given that she was attributing her success to the investment of time and attention by her spouse, I asked how much time had she invested in the development of her staff for them to reach the level of excellence for which she was holding them accountable.

From that point, we were able to discuss resources that could help her to help her team. Frequent follow-up and development of action plans helped to further put this EVP and her team on the path to excellence

---

Know Your Limits

There is always one rare occasion when what was presented as an employee issue, turns out to be a legal issue that moves the resolution outside of the department and the human resources arena. Managers and human resource professionals need to understand where to draw the line when presented with these issues. When illegal actions are involved, seek the necessary professional resources to handle the situation. Unfortunately, I had the opportunity to address several of these issues during my career.

One example that I recall is being contacted by the Drug Enforcement Administration (DEA). An employee of the company had used a prescription pad from one of the physicians in the practice and had written prescriptions for herself at several local pharmacies. The DEA had copies of all the prescriptions, video recordings of the employee picking up the drugs and by the physician's name on the prescription pad, had traced the employee to our organization. When faced with this type of situation, the only thing that you can do is cooperate with the authorities.

On other occasions, you may find yourself dealing with a situation involving someone with unresolved or undiagnosed mental health issues. These may be very serious and can be dangerous if handled in the wrong way.

Dealing with an employee with mental health issues may be difficult to recognize because the illness can manifest in so many different ways throughout their employment. Excessive absenteeism may be the result of PTSD or depression. Unprofessional behavior may be the result of unresolved trauma or abuse.

This is not always the case, but for employees who suffer any of these issues, one wrong word or action can send the employee into a downward spiral. The only way to know which direction to go with these employees is by engaging them in conversation with dignity and respect and listening to what they have to tell you.

The stories below are two of the situations that I was asked to address.

An organization hired me to handle its employee relations issues and told me about an employee at one of the outside entities that were exhibiting unusual behaviors. This employee had been witnessed on several occasions walking backward through her entire shift and standing in frozen positions for several minutes at a time. This employee had also complained to her supervisor that her workers were throwing acid at her legs as she went about her shift.

Previous to my arrival, the employee had been asked to voluntarily seek help from the company's Employee Assistance Program (EAP), which she had done. A quick word here about voluntary EAP referral. Organizations are not privy to any information that is gathered when the employee voluntarily seeks help from an Employee Assistance Program.

I arranged to meet with the employee and her manager to hear the issues and concerns first hand. I listened as the employee explained that she walked backward and stood frozen was her way of watching and preventing her co-workers from throwing the acid on her legs. She voluntarily lifted her pants to show me the evidence of the scars on her legs from the acid attacks. Needless to say, there were no scars.

I told the employee that I was aware of the previous voluntary EAP referral, but I believed that we needed to do another EAP referral, this time as a mandatory referral to ensure that we can understand what is causing her episodes.

The employee was compliant with the referral. The resulting diagnoses and treatment resolved the employee's episodes and she went back to being an effective part of the team.

Other situations take longer to resolve.

After joining another organization, I was told about a young man who had been a superstar in the organization. The young man was smart, out-going, and up and comer in his field.

Unfortunately, as a result of an accident, the young man had suffered a severe head injury. He could no longer fulfill the responsibilities of his job assignment, but the organization was committed to helping him transition into another role. So, as you have guessed, I got to be the one to get him to understand his limitations and move him in another direction.

Over several months, I had the manager set up retraining for the young man. Had his work evaluated by others, and pointed out the errors of his reasoning explained to him. I talked with him about other areas of interest and pointed out skill sets that I recognized during our time together.

Slowly, by building trust with the young man, I made progress, eventually steering him to an assignment that was perfect for him.

CONCLUSON

Employee relations involves using the efforts necessary to create and maintain positive and constructive relationships in the workplace.

Too often managers expect the relationship between the employee and their co-workers or employee and their manager to develop on its own. The manager fails to factor in the experiences and expectations that each employee brings to the workplace that may or may not mesh with what is going on in the work environment.

Particularly in the mind of the new manager, their responsibilities are limited to their staffing needs and meeting organizational goals. Many times, they are unprepared for the effort required to build effective teams and keep personalities in check.

Every type of relationship requires work. It involves putting forth the effort to ensure that each party feels connected and valued for what they bring to the table.

The more seasoned manager may be more aware of the effort necessary to achieve positive outcomes, but the resolution for them can be confusing and emotionally exhausting.

The purpose of this book is to serve as a resource. The information presented is designed to help managers overcome the fear of addressing employee issues. It is also designed to guide the manager to address those issues in a way that demonstrates respect and dignity for the parties involved.

It is my sincere hope that you use The Art of Employee Relations to create your workplace masterpieces!

"Your Notes"

"Your Notes"

DEBORAH A. TULLOS

"Your Notes"

------------------------"Your Notes"---------------------

"Your Notes"

89